Tips from the

OLD HOUSEWIVES

Elizabeth Drury

PAST TIMES®

First published in Great Britain in 2003 by
SJG Publishing for Past Times

Manufactured in Thailand by Imago

Contents

3

"*Some respite to husbands the weather may send,
But housewives' affairs have never an end.*"

Thomas Tusser (1524?–80)
Preface to the Book of Housewifery

Foreword

"Of all those acquirements, which more particularly belong to the feminine character," wrote Mrs Beeton, "there are none which take a higher rank, in our estimation, than such as enter into a knowledge of household duties; for on these are perpetually dependent the happiness, comfort and well-being of a family." Those of a masculine character who prefer to avoid all kinds of domestic responsibility are apt to agree with her description of the role of the housewife.

With the *Book of Household Management* Isabella Beeton helped to invent the Victorian housewife, the woman who knew how everything in the home ought to be, and ought to be done. For generations of women, what they didn't learn from their elders (and by definition, in their own eyes, betters) they found the answer to in Mrs Beeton.

After the First World War, and with the introduction of devices that made running a home a bit easier, a great many housewives had to face up to looking after themselves, with practically nobody to help them. No longer were they simply the mistress and manager of the house but the worker too. The "servant problem", instead of being about what to expect of them – practically and with regard to their moral rectitude – was about how to find them at all.

Some housewives, finding themselves in this situation, were "helpless" in every sense of the word. Mrs Beeton's advice was updated and new books appeared with such titles as *First Aid for the Servantless, Things a Woman Wants to Know, Labour-saving Hints and Ideas for the Home*. They had to learn to be "hands-on".

Here are some of the housewifely notions and tricks that our grandmothers and great-grandmothers might have known – whether they had servants or not. It is reassuring that so much could be done with such ordinary and relatively harmless substances as tea leaves, potato peelings, common salt, lemon juice, and vinegar, though a few of the suggestions are a bit too ingenious, or dangerous, to put to the test. Perhaps, somewhere among them, is the answer to something you have always wondered about or wanted to know. You never can tell.

Kitchen wisdom

And the frugal shopper

The cook is a person of conspicuous importance. If cook is playing up, or has an "off" day, who knows what the consequences might be? She is to be appeased at all costs, especially if the cook is the housewife herself.

The cook in days gone by would have been assisted by a kitchen maid, where such a minion could be afforded. This person was responsible for keeping the kitchen, the areas leading to or adjoining the kitchen and all the cooking utensils in a tip-top state of cleanliness. Her main task, though, was to prepare all the fish, meat and vegetables. Whereas the cook might be applauded and described as a "marvel" or a "treasure", the kitchen maid was the recipient of little praise and much blame.

Provisioning the household

Frugality – a cardinal Victorian virtue – was the name of the game with regard to provisioning the household. Two points to remember: a bargain is not a bargain when you don't need it; and cheap food is not necessarily inferior. And then there's the saying, "Wilful waste brings woeful want". Beware buying too much and having to throw some away (hence the many recipes for leftovers in cookery books).

Mrs Beeton was very hot on getting up early, quoting William Pitt the elder: "If you do not rise early, you can make progress in nothing". This was particularly important when it came to doing the shopping (the fable of the early bird and the worm).

Adulteration (not adultery)

The housewife must employ her eyes and nostrils to test the freshness of produce (almost all of it local, once upon a time) and look out for adulteration of goods by the addition of spurious ingredients.

Fresh fish won't smell of fish. It should have clear eyes and shiny scales. Ask the fishmonger (or the butcher, if you fancy meat) what he's going to eat tonight and you'll know what's worth buying.

There were various known tests for finding out whether goods were as fresh and pure as they were said to be. To assess the quality of sugar burn a little in an iron ladle. Pure sugar burns away completely; impure sugar leaves ash proportionate to the degree of adulteration. Ground coffee, when held in the palm of the hand, should fall apart when the hand is opened. If it sticks together in a lump it is impure and at some stage something has been added. Dip a steel knitting-needle into milk. If the milk drops off slowly it is pure; if it runs off in a hurry it has been diluted with water. Macaroni should break with a crunch. Nutmegs should leak oil when pricked with a pin.

Kitchen maxims

- Arrange the house so that the kitchen is close to an outside door, to where the food is to be consumed and so that smells cannot spread through the house.
- Be clean in your person so as not to contaminate the food.
- Punctuality is an indispensable quality. A cook who loses an hour in the morning will be toiling all day.
- On no account store dairy products near fish or strong smelling food.
- Clear as you go: muddle makes more muddle.
- Never cook by guessing. More money is wasted in this way than by careless shopping and storing.
- Water boils when it gallops, oil when it is still.
- A stew boiled is a stew spoiled.
- Give yourself time to inspect for insects in greens before putting them in soak.

"While statesmen may carve nations, good cooks alone can consolidate them."

Mrs Beeton's Everyday Cookery, 1850

The kitchen range

The range, burning solid fuel, was the glowing heart of the kitchen in the old days. Attention had to be paid to its every whim to prevent paralysis of the entire household.

It would be a mistake to start cleaning the range with the door and window open. The draught would scatter soot everywhere. And close the oven door too. Starting at the top, open the flue doors one by one and sweep down the soot with a flue brush. Sweep out and wash the oven with hot soda water and if the top of the stove is greasy treat it in the same way. When it is thoroughly dry, apply black-lead, moistened with turpentine, to the black parts. Polish when the stove begins to warm up. If the steel mouldings are badly stained rub them with moistened ashes, finishing off with emery paper.

Tea and its leaves

Tea, even in the days of teabags, definitely tastes better when it is made with soft water, which softens and opens out the tea leaves. And it is apparently well known that for tea to be as free as it can be from injurious properties it should be poured into the cup first, before the milk, as scalding tea poured into the milk causes the tannin to form a leathery and indigestible drink (Contrariwise, in making coffee the milk should be poured in first.)

When you use a silver teapot and the tea party is over, dry the inside and put a lump of sugar in it. This will drink up any remaining moisture and prevent the teapot from becoming musty.

When putting away a silver teapot or coffee-pot make sure that a little stick is put across the top, under the lid, to allow fresh air to get in and prevent that musty smell. Should this simple precaution be forgotten, fill the pot with boiling water and drop in a red-hot cinder. Close the lid and leave it for a moment or two for wonders to be worked.

Never throw away tea leaves. You will be surprised to see how useful they are for cleaning all manner of things, from carpets to black suede shoes, either as leaves or as a liquid made from the dregs.

On saucepans

Should you by any chance, in forgetful mode, boil a saucepan dry, fill it with salt and water and forget about it again for a few hours. Then bring the liquid slowly to boiling-point. The blackened contents can then be removed much more easily. Another method is to fill it with wood ash and let it stand for a while.

Saucepans should never be put away with their lids on. The old-fashioned way was to hang them in the kitchen with their faces turned away from you and to the wall.

Don't get cross with a saucepan when the knob comes off its lid. Find a small cork, put a screw through the hole in the lid from underneath and screw the cork into it.

Kettles

The old way of cleaning a kettle was to boil in it a few potato peelings. A fur coat would not form if a small stone marble or an oyster shell were kept in it.

Copper culture

No self-respecting kitchen should be without its display of copper. A gleaming row of polished copper pans used to occupy pride of place. Strong they were, and admired for their longevity as well as their appearance, but they took an inordinate amount of time to clean.

To create a fine polish, malt vinegar and silver sand in equal quantities were mixed together to form a paste. This was applied to the surface with one cloth and rubbed with another till it glowed. To allow the copper to become coated with poisonous verdigris (green copper rust) could be interpreted as murderous negligence. The linings of utensils had to be tinned to make them safe for cooking.

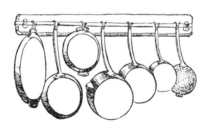

That smells fishy

Tea leaves come to the rescue when you have a saucepan that smells of fish. Tip the dregs from the teapot straight into the pan and cover them with water. After a few minutes rinse them out and fishy history will be forgotten. Another way is to fill the saucepan with cold water and a little vinegar and then bring it to the boil.

To banish the smell of fish from silverware add a spoonful of mustard to the washing-up water.

Peppery prudence

Put a dried pea among ground pepper and it will stop the holes in the lid from clogging up (and a few grains of rice in the salt will do the same).

Washing up

This is usually looked upon as one of the humblest and most tiresome of household tasks and is therefore apt to be performed without much thought or method. Actually, it is a job that requires careful planning to save time and the onset of boredom and carelessness.

Silver that has been touched by vinegar or egg should be rubbed between the finger and thumb with fine table salt before it is washed. (Because, with vinegar and eggs, the silver turns black a bone spoon is sometimes used for eating a boiled egg, and a wooden spoon for pickles and wooden servers for salad with vinegar in the dressing.)

Tea stains on teacups is a familiar annoyance. They can be removed quite easily by rubbing the surface vigorously with salt and water. Particularly obstinate cases used to be treated with bone dust and water (bone dust formerly obtainable from any chemist).

Glasses that have been used for milk should be rinsed in cold water before they are washed up.

"A woman's work and washing of dishes
is never at an end"

Hints for the helpless

Vinegar in the washing-up water removes grease, brightens glass and china and acts as a disinfectant.

Clean aluminium with sand and hot water.

Put thin glassware into the washing-up water sideways and no matter how hot the water is the glasses won't crack.

Decanters are best cleaned by shaking around a mixture of crushed eggshells, vinegar, tea leaves and water.

Half fill a milk bottle with warm soapy water and add a teaspoonful of uncooked rice. Then give it a good shake.

Bottles that have had vinegar in them can be purified by filling them with potato peelings topped up with water, then allowing them to stand until the peelings ferment.

For stained water bottles chop up extra fine some raw potato. Add a little vinegar and put the potato and vinegar into the bottle. Shake it very well, add a little water and again shake, then rinse it all out. (Tea leaves with salt and vinegar do just as well.)

Pass dry breadcrumbs through a mincing machine before washing it.

What you need to know about eggs

The following, very scientific experiment will tell you the age of an egg. Put six ounces of salt in a large glass and fill it with water. When the salt has dissolved drop in the egg. If the egg is one day old it sinks to the bottom; if any older it does not reach the bottom. If it is three days old it sinks to only just below the surface; five days old or more it floats and the older it is the more it protrudes out of the water.

Eggs direct from the nest (new laid and free-range, in today's language) are said to be less rich and appetizing than when they are a day or two old. For invalids a day-old egg is meant to be just the thing. Sometimes they burst when they are being boiled and this is because they have too much air in them. Pricking one end with a needle before eggs are put into the water stops this happening. And if they're already cracked when you want to boil them try wrapping them up in a twist of tissue paper. You shouldn't lose any of the contents that way.

For some reason eggs covered with boiling water and allowed to stand for five minutes were once thought to be more nourishing and more easily digested than an egg put in boiling water and cooked for three and a half minutes. Why should this be so?

A spoonful of vinegar will help set a poached egg.

People who have difficulty separating eggs could try breaking them into a funnel: the white runs through and the yolk stays behind. Should the yolk break and droplets find their way into the white, dip a cloth in warm water, wring it dry and touch the yolk with a corner of it. The yolk should by rights adhere to the cloth.

A duck's egg is equal to two small hen's eggs.

Add a pinch of salt to the whites of eggs when you are beating them. You will be surprised how much better they whip.

Egg white comes in useful for making meringues but also for repairing torn books, for gluing on small pieces of wood chipped off furniture, for cleaning and renovating a black straw hat and leather chairs and sofas.

Household chores

Everyday tasks about the home

Housework, the repetitive and never-ending business of keeping the house clean and preparing for the events of the day, used to be delegated to a housemaid, supervised in well-to-do households by a housekeeper, or to a parlour maid. In time these most often were replaced by a "daily" or a lady who "comes in" and "does", if not by the housewife herself (rarely the househusband). She was assisted by machines such as vacuum cleaners that were disapprovingly described by people who didn't use them as "newfangled".

Suitably dressed for the job

An overall should be worn for housework, preferably with eight pockets for the innumerable articles that have to be carried about. This was one piece of advice given to the novice at doing it all herself. Sleeves must be innocent of buttons, which might make a mark on surfaces and make them look as though they had been scratched by a cat. A print or chintz sun bonnet is useful for protecting the hair from dust.

20

Spring cleaning

This is something to be feared, being very disruptive to the household. Some people, especially husbands, would move out to a hotel while it was going on.

Spring cleaning has been described as the most beneficial domestic operation of the year. It represents a rigorous pursuit of cleanliness and cleanliness, as we all should know, is next to godliness. Principally it involves turning out every room in the house, one by one. Anything that needs repairing should be sent to the mender's so that is helpfully out of the way for the duration, and much better fitted to take its place in the scheme of things when it comes back. It is also a throwing-away opportunity of no-longer-wanted possessions — particularly satisfactory if they are the property of someone else in the household.

Smug housewives would say that their daily cleaning routine makes such an upheaval quite unnecessary.

Front door

First impressions

Make a shield of stiff cardboard by cutting a hole the same shape and size as the surround of a knob or knocker. A slit in the cardboard will make it easier to put in place. If you don't lose it you can use the shield for years to avoid getting polish on the wood.

Brass door furniture tarnishes very quickly so you could take the precaution of rubbing a little furniture polish, vaseline or olive oil over it after polishing (only a little or else greasy finger-marks will be left on the next thing that is touched). Twice a week should be enough.

After washing a doorstep, paint it over with a mixture made from half a pint of skimmed milk and a little quicklime. This dries so firmly that it won't be washed off easily. A visitor approaching the house will be immediately impressed.

Parlour

Fireplaces

A housemaid, first thing in the morning in times gone by, would see to the fires. Long before the family was awake she was on her knees in front of the fireplaces, starting with the parlour. She had a bucket for the ashes or cinders, and in true frugal fashion both ashes and cinders were kept and used for some household purpose. If by any chance soot or coal dust found its mysterious way onto the carpet she would quickly cover it with salt and brush it off with a stiff brush. It was important never to wet the stain with water.

One of her main tasks was to set to with the black-lead. Black-lead, made with lamp-black, could be bought as a solid block and a piece broken off and mixed with water or turpentine. It was put on with a brush, allowed to dry and then rubbed till it gleamed.

To prevent the fire bars turning red there was a curious recommendation that they should be rubbed with a raw onion or weak treacle and water before they were black-leaded. Normally, they were rubbed with emery paper and then polished – ideally with a smooth pebble.

Mantelpieces and hearths

A marble mantelpiece can to be made to look as good as new by treating it thus. Take two parts of common washing soda, one part of finely powdered chalk, one part of pumice stone and mix it all together, then sift it through muslin. Mix this with water to make a paste and rub it in. To give the mantelpiece a glossy surface wash it with fuller's earth and hot water.

Stone or marble hearths need to be rubbed with pumice stone and soap, then rinsed. Tiles, after being washed, should be wiped over with paraffin.

To clean steel fire-irons

Scrape a little bath brick or emery powder into a saucer and add enough paraffin to wet it, then apply the mixture to the steel with a linen cloth and rub well. (Don't use a flannel cloth as this will absorb the paraffin and stop the abrasive doing its work.) Polish with a chamois leather and dry whiting (powdered chalk). By this method rust will be eradicated from steel that has suffered from neglect. (To get rid of the smell of paraffin on your hands rub them with dry sawdust before washing them.)

Straw and cane

Puppies before they are house-trained are the enemies of straw matting, which likes to be washed as seldom as possible. When it does become necessary wash just a small bit at a time with salt and water – half a pint of salt to four of water – and dry it as quickly as possible. The salt prevents the matting from turning a rather nasty yellow.

Choose a fine day when you decide to pay a cane seat some attention. Take it out into the open – and possibly fresh – air and wash it with lukewarm water in which salt and a lump of soda has been dissolved. Rinse it well and let it dry before giving it a light coating of linseed oil. The cane will be stiffened by this method and, though the chair will still creak when sat upon, it will be less likely to let you down.

A new broom

It's obvious, really, that if you nail a fold of thick cloth, velvet or india-rubber round its head, it won't injure the paintwork and furniture. But the head has to be made of wood, to take the nails.

Caring for carpets

Before vacuum cleaners, or even carpet sweepers, were invented leftovers in the teapot were rinsed several times, squeezed dry, thrown into a jar with a little salt and sprinkled over carpets before they were swept with a stiff brush. This helped to keep down the dust and prevent it from flying around the room. (I wouldn't take much notice of the person who suggested using

grass cuttings, but shredded newspaper soaked in water and sprinkled over the carpet seems a reasonable alternative to tea leaves.) Before the tea-leaf ceremony began all the furniture had to be covered with dust sheets.

Wiping carpets over with a cloth wrung out in ammonia and water was a way of keeping carpets looking fresh. Always brush a carpet the way of the pile, otherwise the dust will be brushed *in* rather than *out*.

To get rid of a stain, mix fuller's earth and boiling water to a thick paste and spread it thickly over the mark, leaving it there for twenty-four hours. Then brush it off. This usually works.

When you decide to rearrange your room and find that a piece of furniture has left footprints on the carpet, don't despair. Lay a wet towel, folded in two, over the place and steam it gently with a hot iron. This should lift the pile to the level of the rest of the carpet.

For worn rugs a trick known to dealers in antique or at least second-hand carpets might save a pound or two. Choose the predominant colour, match to it a dye (or a felt-tip pen) and treat the bare threads. Nobody ought to be looking at their shoes, the only reason to notice the deception.

To stop the edge of a carpet or mat from curling make some very thick starch and paste it along the edge. Place some brown paper over the starched part and dry it with a fairly hot iron. To repair the worn edge of a rug put some strong blind cord along it and work over and over the cord with yarn of an appropriate colour.

Remember that the more often a floor rug is shaken the longer it will live. Dirt trapped underneath it grinds down the threads.

Music while you work

Polishing a wooden floor in the old days might involve first scattering steel shavings over it, the process of sweeping them up being mildly abrasive. Using a broom covered with a rough cloth, a mixture of beeswax and turpentine was applied and then rubbed with a block of wood (or, even better because they are heavier, a couple of bricks tied together) wound round with thick layers of flannel. The floors of the galleries in the Louvre used to be polished by an army of men working in time to music supplied by a government fiddler. This kind of labour is slightly more interesting if it is seen as a form of aerobic exercise and done to a rhythm. It can of course be done kneeling, using grease of the elbow.

Traditional floor polish is made by putting half a pound of beeswax cut into fine strips in an enamel bowl and setting this in a saucepan of hot water over a low heat. Stir until the wax has melted, take the bowl out and add one and a half pints of turpentine. Blend it well. An economical floor polish can be made from candle ends, melted down, with an equal proportion of turpentine added; the wicks to be retrieved and discarded.

The wise housewife makes sure that the floor is never polished under a rug as this would encourage the rug to slip.

A dusty answer

The widespread belief that fresh air is essential to health is a nuisance as opening the window lets in grime. Florence Nightingale was actually very against dusting as she said that flapping around a room with a cloth was simply a way of redistributing dirt and was unhygienic. She was all in favour of wiping everything with a damp cloth – except for the pictures.

Housemaids going about their work efficiently used to wash their dusters at the end of every day. Ironing makes them smoother, and better at picking up the dust. Putting a few drops of paraffin on them makes the dust cling, and it's quite good for the furniture as well.

A feather duster was a fashionable accessory for reaching into high and difficult places

"Dirt is bad, but Dust is deadly"

Wallpaper, to clean and repair

First of all, brush the wall with a perfectly clean soft brush or blow away the top layer of dust with bellows. Then divide a stale loaf of white bread into large pieces. Take the crust in your hand and rub the paper downwards in firm clear strokes, using a new piece of bread each time. The accrued grime will attach itself to

the bread and fall to the floor as dirty crumbs. It will look as good as new if properly done. (Breadcrumbs can also be used for cleaning chintz and distempered surfaces.)

If you ever need to patch wallpaper, to hide a stain or injury to the decorations, tear the paper irregularly and the edges will be less noticeable than with a rectangular piece. If the original paper has darkened a bit with old age, give it some tea in the form of a wipe-over.

Pictures, to hang

A picture is seen to advantage if its centre is at the same level as the average pair of eyes, between five foot and five foot six inches from the floor. You may, of course, think it would be an advantage not to see it at all well, in which case hang it on a wall away from the light, on a window wall for example, if there is no other source of light.

The most conspicuous position in a room is over a mantelpiece (whether or not it faces the light). Allow eight to ten inches above the top of the shelf so that there's room for ornaments – and invitations, in case you're invited to a party.

On the subject of windows

For cleaning windows newspaper comes in handy. Mix equal quantities of water, paraffin and methylated spirits in a bottle and shake it thoroughly. Rub the windows with the liquid using a rag and then polish them with a wad of newspaper. This was the way it used to be done.

Rub the sash cords of your windows with soap and they will last ten times as long as they would otherwise do and will run much more smoothly.

Best-ever furniture polish

Housewives, or their housemaids, always used to make their own polish, and it really isn't all that difficult to do. All you need is two ounces of beeswax, a dessertspoonful of turpentine and a tablespoonful of wine vinegar. Melt the beeswax in an enamel bowl over heat, as in the recipe for floor polish. Add the turpentine and then the vinegar, stirring all the while. Once it has turned into a smooth liquid pour it into a screw-top jar, making sure that it is airtight. Keep the jar somewhere cool.

Only use a very little polish and rub it in hard to get rid of the rings made by unhelpful guests who put down their glasses without thinking. This is a better way of getting rid of them (the rings, not the guests) than using equal quantities of linseed oil and turpentine, which is an alternative.

The polish would be an excellent thing to make for a charity fair or the church fête: Ms Somebody's Original Best-ever Furniture Polish.

To remove scratches and polish ebonized furniture, paint with Indian ink, smoooth with fine sandpaper and paint again. When it has dried, smear linseed oil over it and then apply best-ever furniture polish.

Mirror, mirror

Rub the glass with methylated spirits and give it a final polish using a chamois leather and whiting.

A gilded frame – and the gilding on any furniture – should be washed with water in which an onion has been boiled, then dried with a soft cloth.

Preserving and polishing pianos

A piano likes the same kind of atmosphere as most house-plants. It needs a little moisture so that the sounding-board doesn't dry out and shrink, and the piano lose its tone. Especially with central heating, it is a good idea to put a tall bottle of water with a narrow neck inside the case at the bottom of an upright piano with a "wick" made of newspaper.

To clean ivory keys, rub each one with a cloth dampened with eau-de-Cologne and dipped in whiting. Then polish with an old silk handkerchief. Stains can be removed by rubbing the keys over with a paste of whiting and hydrogen peroxide.

Lampshades

Lampshades need to be cleaned every week (as everyone knows). Using a soft brush (an out of work shaving-brush for instance), the best way is to deal with the inside first. Then the outside, brushing downwards.

Chandeliers

Chandeliers need to be washed twice a year, in the spring and the autumn. Cover the floor underneath with a dust sheet and fill a bucket with soapy water, adding a dessertspoonful of ammonia. Find a stepladder of the right height and use this rather than trusting a chair (which probably wouldn't be high enough anyway). The drops have to be washed one by one, and you need to mark where you began in some way so that you don't go round and round — and round. Start with the top tier and work downwards. Wipe two or three drops with a soap-filled cloth, then dry them with another cloth. Put the wet cloth back into the soapy water and squeeze it before starting on the next few drops. The most tiresome part of the job is moving the stepladder every few minutes. Don't try to stretch too far or there might be a disaster.

Oil lamps

The first piece of disappointing news is that if paraffin lamps are used regularly they need to be given a thorough clean once a week. The next is that once a month they need to be taken to pieces completely. The burners should be boiled in water containing some soda, the founts washed out with soapy water and allowed to dry altogether before they are used again. When replacing the oil, strain it by putting a piece of muslin inside the funnel or a small wad of cotton wool.

Never fill a lamp quite full of oil. When the cold oil is carried into a warm room it will expand and run over, and then the lamp is unfairly blamed for leaking.

Always soak the wicks in vinegar for quarter of an hour before you use them, then hang them up to dry. After that they will last longer and give a steadier, brighter light. To make a chimney absolutely fireproof, before using it for the first time put it in a pan of cold water and bring the water gradually to the boil. Let it boil for quarter of an hour and then leave it to cool.

Dining room

Table talk

Food must at the very least look enticing, especially if the taste is in danger of being unremarkable — on one of those famous "off" days for the cook, or even on her day off, for instance — and the table arrangements must be elegant.

No table can look attractive unless it is symmetrical. A tablecloth laid evenly, with the centre fold lying in a straight line down the length of an oblong table, a space of twenty-four inches allowed for each person's accommodation, the disposition of salt and pepper (a salt cellar between every two persons) and the correct and strictly geometrical laying up of the table with china, glass, knives, spoons and forks were details that no housewife attentive to her family and guests (and her own reputation) could afford to neglect. It would be noticed at once if the silver were set more — or less — than half an inch from the edge of the table or silver and glasses not placed in the order in which they were to be used.

A cunning ploy to disguise a single blemish on a white cloth is to cover it with a piece of white stamp paper. This won't show and it'll come off in the wash.

To hand dishes at an inconvenient height or at an angle dangerous to clothing, and with the free hand resting casually on the back of the chair, is wrong. Servants – permanent or hired for the occasion – must be instructed to avoid this. Definitely to be discouraged is conspicuous evidence of a servant listening to the dinner-table conversation (though he or she is, of course) and, horror of horrors, joining in, to correct or contradict.

As far as table decorations are concerned, spotlessly white napkins folded into complicated shapes such as the Rose and Star are bound to impress; and so might tasteful arrangements of flowers, but they must not be strongly scented. Asparagus fronds and maidenhair ferns had their moment.

When entertaining some "lion" who has distinguished himself in a particular walk of life there was once thought to be a case for adopting the bizarre rather than the beautiful: a table arranged as an aerodrome with aeroplanes hovering over it, perhaps, for someone famous for his flying exploits.

Curtain calls

First-time homemakers need to be made aware that curtains reaching down to the floor encourage a shallow room to look taller than it really is. This is particularly desirable in a dining-room, where from time to time – if the housewife is a conscientious, or ambitious, hostess – a number of people might be invited to gather under the same ceiling.

Heavy fabrics make curtains difficult to pull. When they are suspended from rings they can be helped on their way by rubbing the pole with paraffin.

Clearing the air

In the old days cigar smoking in well-to-do households was a masculine occupation that took place only in the dining room after the ladies had withdrawn (to gossip, etc.). Here, the curtains were particularly susceptible to infection by tobacco smoke.

To get rid of the fumes (and who wants to breathe them in, particularly the morning after?), they used to put a pint of hot water and three tablespoonfuls of ammonia in a bowl and leave it there for several hours. Alternatively, they sprinkled some dry coffee grounds into a shovel of red-hot cinders.

Wax, wicks and candlesticks

One way of stopping the wax overflowing onto the holder and cooling in grotesque shapes is to coat the candle with varnish. This forms a "cup" as the candle burns down, and the molten wax is contained.

If you do get wax on the tablecloth warm a knife over the flame, slip it under the wax and lift it off.

Char the wick in advance and the candle will be easier to light when dinner is ready. Always light a candle by holding the match to the side of the wick and not over the top, and never try to light it from another candle or from the fire as it is bound to drip on something. A wick that is too long is starved of fuel and therefore difficult to light, so trim it close.

A wick soaked in vinegar will never smoke, or so it is said

When a candle is too small for its holder, some people wrap a wad of paper or silver paper round the base. A less noticeable method of dealing with the problem is to dip the end in hot water and it will then be soft enough to ram down into the holder and mould to the right size.

Pantry

Servicing silver

In a fully staffed establishment the silver used to be cleaned after each time it was used. And when it wasn't needed it was wrapped in tissue paper and put away. One part plate powder to two parts silversmith's rouge were the traditional constituents of silver polish, or whiting mixed to a paste with ammonia. To get right into the crevices, particularly of embossed work, an old toothbrush has always been found a useful weapon, and a soft brush specially made for silver to bring up the shine. Finish the polishing with a chamois leather. Rub mildewed silver with whiting mixed with paraffin before you try to give it a gleam.

They used to say that it was a good idea to keep a piece of camphor with silver that wasn't being used all the time to prevent it tarnishing.

Knife skills

To clean non-stainless steel knives, for those unfortunate enough not to have a knife-machine, dip a cork in dry coffee grounds, fine sand, salt or crushed charcoal and rub hard. Or, get your hands on an old and small piece of Brussels carpet, fold it in two and sprinkle it liberally with knife powder. Insert the knife and rub vigorously.

A trick, if the blades have gone rusty, is to stick them in garden soil or a flower pot for a couple of hours and then rub them well with a damp cloth dipped in ashes.

To clean ivory handles and prevent them turning yellow rub them with a cut lemon and then wash them in soapy water. Fix a blade that has distanced itself from the handle by filling the hole with a mixture of resin and brick dust, heating the tang of the knife and pressing it home.

Bedroom

Bedmaking for beginners

A grown-up man exhales at least three pints of moisture in every twenty-four hours and during the night much of that goes into the bedding, said Florence Nightingale. No wonder, then, that it was thought so important to strip a bed (women's and children's as well as men's) and air the bedclothes every day – except on foggy days, with the window open. The bottom sash of the bedroom window *must* be closed by sunset.

In any doubt as to whether a bed is damp? Put a mirror between the sheets and if, after a few minutes, the glass is misty you know for sure that it is. It used to be said that when going away for a couple of weeks (and turning off the heating) you would find your bed quite dry on returning if you had been wise enough to leave a blanket on top after the bed had been made. Only the blanket then needed airing.

To wash pillows, spill the feathers into a muslin bag larger than the original ticking case (you might need two pairs of hands for this) and sew it up. Wash in a bathful of soapy water and rinse thoroughly. Squeeze the muslin bag gently and hang it out to dry before putting the feathers back into the – preferably new – ticking case. Clean pillows are more of a necessity than a luxury. Think of the germs, and what if someone's cried into it!

To fluff up a blanket after it has been washed, peg it out on the washing line and beat it with an old tennis racquet.

Clean old iron bedsteads with a cloth damped with paraffin or rub them with furniture cream.

Bugs in the bed: see Domestic nuisances

Silent nights

There is nothing more annoying – and spooking – than a creaking bedroom door if you are trying to sleep, and nothing more of a giveaway if you have a nocturnal agenda. Rub the hinges with a lead pencil or a lump of lard.

Bathroom

The bath and other receptacles

Marks on an enamelled bath can be caused by the clotting of soap in hard water and the evaporation of drops of water allowed to remain on the surface. To get rid of them, try using a cloth moistened with paraffin and dipped in salt, and rubbing the place. The result should astonish you. Don't forget to rinse the bath with plenty of hot water before you use it.

Coat the bathroom mirror with glycerine and you won't have to look at yourself through a fog.

A dose of soda and common salt is the answer to a basin or bath so clogged up with soap that the water won't run away. Force the mixture down the plughole and leave it for half an hour. Then pour down a kettle's worth of boiling water.

Verdigris on brass taps (indicating a bad housemaid or the housewife's neglectful ways) can be removed with an old toothbrush dipped in ammonia. Another way of getting rid of mineral deposits is to smother the taps with a cloth soaked in hot vinegar and leave them like that for an hour or two, then wipe or scrub.

Half a cup of borax thrown into the lavatory pan, swished around with a brush and left for the night is quite good enough to clean it, especially if a dose of washing soda is administered every now and again. Soapy water was usually all that was used before specialist detergents and disinfectants – and "ducks" – were invented. After all, a lavatory that is frequented is constantly being flushed out with water.

For modesty's sake

In the interests of propriety, there are often windows that we would prefer barred to the gaze of passers-by. To frost a window take a jam jar one third full of gum arabic and add a little hot water. Let this soak for some hours and when the gum has quite dissolved add the same quantity of Epsom salts. Then stand the jam jar in a basin of hot water and stir until the salts have quite dissolved. Apply the mixture quickly to the glass with a brush (camel hair, naturally).

Potted instructions for washing and cleaning

Brass
: Mix emery powder to a paste with paraffin, then polish with an old piece of velvet. For a quick shine breathe hard on it and polish.

Bronze
: $\frac{1}{16}$ ounce lavender oil, $1\frac{1}{2}$ ounces water, 1 ounce alcohol. Mix and apply with a sponge. No rubbing required.

Felt
: Also velour. Rub with hot bran then brush with a soft brush.

Hog's hair
: A walnut-sized piece of soda or a few drops of ammonia in boiling water. Dip in the bristles of a pen brush – or hair brush – until clean. Shake well.

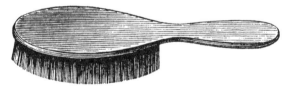

Ivory
: Make a paste of sal volatile and olive oil. Rub it on with a wash-leather. Leave to dry in the sun. Brush off and polish.

Leather	Wash leather furniture and suitcases with soap and warm water, rinse with cold water. When dry coat with white of egg , and when the egg is dry polish with a soft duster. To prevent the leather from cracking give it a vaseline treatment from time to time.
Mother-of-pearl	Wash with a mixture of powdered whiting and cold water.
Ormolu	Rub ornaments with whiting moistened with gin, brush off with a very soft brush and polish with a chamois leather.
Papier-mâché	Wash with cold water, dredge with flour and polish.
Pewter	Blend equal proportions of methylated spirits and whiting to form a paste. Rub it in hard and then polish with a chamois leather.
Tin	Polish by rubbing with an onion after dipping in soda and water.
Zinc	Clean with hot soap and water, then polish with kerosene. Or use lime and water mixed to the consistency of cream.

Secrets of the laundry room

What to do and what not to do

The housewife probably benefited from the invention of labour-saving appliances to a greater extent in dealing with the washing – when it was done at home – than in almost any other area of her responsibilities. Take sheets: it's hard to imagine what a business it was putting them in a tub to soak (in water to which soda or borax had been dissolved), rinsing and transferring the heavy, water-laden articles to the copper, boiling and rubbing them by hand, rinsing and adding the right amount of blue to the water to counteract yellowing, rinsing again and wringing them, drying (preferably out of doors so that the sun could do its bleaching trick), then mangling or ironing, folding and last of all airing them. And after that the copper had to be scrubbed with fine sand and soap ready for the next time.

A conscientious housewife's airing cupboard would be her pride and joy, and a measure of the quality of her housekeeping. All the linen, beautifully aired and ironed, was arranged neatly on the shelves and and numbered so that it was used in a particular order and no item could complain of unfair usage. A young woman traditionally brought the household linen to a marriage. It was bought beforehand, embroidered and marked with her new initials. Still, in the twentieth century, it was believed that hand towels and napkins, and even some of the sheets, tablecloths and towels, would last a lifetime. But that depended on how kindly they were treated.

Clothes and delicate items needed their own special treatment. For example, it was advisable to rinse brown and red silk in water with salt in it, mauves, blues and greens in slightly vinegary water; and to fold shirts and things so that the buttons faced inwards before putting them in the wringer.

The clue to a good wash is to use soft water – and the best is rainwater, specially if it is from the country and has been strained through a piece of muslin. Lime or borax was sometimes added to the water to soften it.

Leftover soap suds could always be saved for washing floors, steps or the verandah, or for watering the roses.

The washerwoman's week

"They that wash on Monday have all the week to dry;
They that wash on Tuesday are not so much awry;
They that wash on Wednesday are not so much to blame;
They that wash on Thursday wash for shame;
They that wash on Friday wash for need;
And they that wash on Saturday
Oh, they're sluts indeed."

Blue for linen

Made with aniline blue, or china blue and oxalic acid, this was used in the rinse to maintain the whiteness of whites. It was sometimes helpful to add milk to the tub when using hard water as it stopped the linen blueing unevenly.

Eggy linen

Hot or boiling water would set the stain until it is all but permanent. Soak the tablecloth or napkin, or a messy breakfaster's shirt, in cold water before you wash it.

Inky linen

An old recipe for households where someone writes essays or letters in bed: most ink stains on sheets and pillowcases can be removed by rubbing with a slice of juicy lemon or with a ripe tomato cut in half and then sponged with cold rainwater. Another idea, which can be used for ironmould as well, is to cover the offending spot with milk and then common salt. Leave this until the blemish seems to have disappeared before washing.

Best way to wash chintz?

Whoever was the first to think of using rice to wash chintz curtains and covers? This is what was recommended that the careful housewife should do. Take two pounds of rice and boil it in two gallons of water until soft, then pour all of it into a tub to cool. Dunk the article to be washed and use the granules of rice as if it were soap, rubbing the fabric until the dirt disappears.

When you have a moment, repeat the process of boiling up two pounds of rice in two gallons of water but this time strain the rice and mix it with fresh warm water. Wash the chintz in this. Then, put it in the water in which the second lot of rice was cooked. This liquid acts as starch and gives a surface gloss. Don't on any account iron the chintz but rather rub it with a smooth stone.

Best way to wash lace

A small length of it, that is. Put the lace in a wide-necked bottle (a milk bottle would be fine if you can find a cork or stopper that will fit tightly into the top). Fill it three-quarters full with warm soapy water and put in the lace. Shake the bottle gently backwards and forwards, as a precaution holding one hand over the top. Rinse in the bottle with first warm and then cold water.

Fruit stains on table linen

Now this is a very risky method of dealing with tablecloths and napkins marked by fruit juice. Draw the stained part very tightly

over a large round bowl or bucket. Stand on a chair and from a great height pour boiling water onto the stain until it disappears. Use a long-spouted gardener's can or you may burn your arm.

Powdered starch applied instantly, left until it has dried and then brushed off, or a dose of salt and lemon juice, might be a less adventurous alternative.

Rhubarb to the rescue

For removing ironmould rhubarb juice is one of the best agents. Cut a stick of rhubarb into chunks and put them in a saucepan with a little water. Boil briskly for a couple of minutes and then hold the stained linen in the concoction and afterwards rinse in cold water.

"Linen often to water, soon to tatter"

The necessity of marking linen

When the household linen is collected by a man in a van and taken to a commercial laundry it behoves every householder to mark the linen in case it is inadvertently exchanged for someone else's. It's not worth taking the chance that sheets and pillowcases of rather better quality than yours will be delivered back to you.

It used to be thought that colds, Bronchitis and even Asthma were communicated by the laundry doing a bit of redistributing.

Starch

Table linen should be only lightly starched. If it is too stiff the corners of a tablecloth, instead of falling in natural folds, will stand out in an awkward fashion and napkins will feel like cardboard. Adding a piece of candle wax to starch gives the linen a smooth, shiny appearance. A way of avoiding using starch altogether used to be to add a tablespoonful of methylated spirits to the last rinse. This too gives the linen a good gloss.

Collars stiff and soft

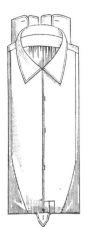

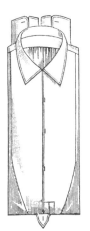

Someone, in the days when men's collars came separate from the bodies of shirts, had a good idea for keeping them round in shape and stiff. Place a small round cake tin in the oven and put the collars in it as they are ironed — but only for a minute or two.

For super-stiff collars, and cuffs as well, dip them in cold starch and iron while damp. Next dip a soft cloth into some French chalk and rub it onto the article on the right side. Lastly rub a piece of white curd soap over the chalk and iron it, again on the right side. The glaze will look like porcelain.

Tricks of ironing

Stand on a cushion to stop your feet getting tired.

As everyone knows, you can't iron silk successfully if it's dry. So, sprinkle the article with water and roll it up tightly in a towel at least an hour before you attempt the task.

Bed- and table-linen (real linen or cotton) is always folded the same way when it has been ironed. It is along the crease that the material wears thin and eventually out. If, after a while, you were to cut off half an inch from one side and hem it, the fold would appear in a different place. To double the normal lifespan of linen fold it one week by the hem and the next week by the selvedge.

To iron lace cover it with clean white tissue paper. Silk will iron up like new if a little methylated spirits has been added to the rinsing water, and it's always best to roll the article up in a dry towel after washing rather than hanging it up – or out – to dry as it needs to be slightly and evenly damp for ironing .

Tricks to avoid ironing

After you have washed, and probably starched, lace curtains hang them up while they are still wet at the window where they belong. If it can be done, run a heavy stick or pole through the hem at the bottom. With a bit of luck they should look as if they had been ironed.

With a cooker such as an Aga you can try folding bed linen carefully while it is still damp and draping it over the top to dry. The result isn't perfect, but you might just get away with it. And try spreading hankerchiefs quite flat on a mirror while they're still wet. (But do you have one to hand at the right moment?)

Scorch injuries

What is to be done when the telltale mark of carelessness spoils a newly laundered article? They used to say that scorch marks could be removed by spreading over them a paste made from the juice of two onions, half an ounce of white soap, two ounces of fuller's earth and half a pint of vinegar. These ingredients had to be mixed together, well boiled and then allowed to cool before the paste could be applied to the injured place.

Knacks and makeshifts

A basketful of housewifely hints

Thrift was one of the acknowledged virtues of the housewife of old. It is not surprising that so much advice was given on how to make and how to recycle and rejuvenate almost everything you can think of. There was an afterlife for the merest morsel of fabric, metal or wood. Worn-out brooms were turned into hearth brushes, shaving brushes into brushes for oiling the sewing-machine, candle ends into economical polish for stained floors, biscuit-tin lids (with wire stretched from side to side) into toasters for gas fires, the top of an old grandfather clock into a medicine chest.

Buttoned up

To sew the button on a coat or on some thick material put a match on top, across the holes in the button (leaving room for the needle), and sew over it. Take away the match and wind the thread round and round the limp shank (or stalk) until it is thick and strong.

Darn it and patch

Darning and patching are two of the most neglected accomplishments of the ideal housewife, the most rigorous test of old-fashioned domestic economy.

Steal the thread for darning from the material itself, pulling out a strand from where it won't be noticed – from the hem, perhaps.

Leave a small loop at either end of a darn with wool and never double the wool.

To thread a darning needle for wool quickly, pass the two ends of a short cotton thread through the needle, then slip the wool through the loop of the thread. Pull the thread through the eye of the needle and your wool comes with it. This will rescue you from several annoying moments.

Patching is best done with a sewing machine, which flattens the material as you work.

"Patch by patch is good housewifery, but patch upon patch is plain beggary"

Knitting hints

For socks and stockings knit mercerised silk or thread with the wool for the heels and toes, the parts that wear out first, and the article will live longer.

Wool used to be bought in skeins and it was up to the knitter to turn them into manageable balls for knitting. Someone else would hold the skein stretched between the two hands, helpfully moving from side to side as the wool was wound. That someone often found it quite a boring job. It could perfectly well be done by turning a chair upside down on another chair and putting the wool round the four legs.

To estimate roughly the amount of wool that is needed to knit a garment take a similar one and weigh it.

To mend lace curtains

Wash and iron the curtain and leave it on the ironing-board. Dip a piece of plain net (whatever the pattern of the original) in starch and squeeze it dry, then lay it over the hole and iron till dry. The edges of the hole should be drawn together as much as possible with thread .

The useful cotton reel

Wooden, of course. Make pegs for doors or cupboards by inserting a long screw or nail into an empty cotton reel and placing it where wanted. A coat of paint gives a less random look. Similarly, a cotton reel can be screwed or nailed to the floor to stop a door opening too far.

Old stiff collars

Don't throw them away. You can cut them up to make luggage labels that are far stronger than paper ones.

Old army puttees

Do you have some of these in the attic or put away somewhere in case they come in useful in some future military engagement? If you're sure you won't need them again you could make them into a mat. Damp and iron the puttees, then cut them into strips of equal length. Divide them in half and lay one lot of the strips crossways over the other, interlacing them. Finish off the edges with binding.

Uncommon species of shoe tree

Fill a pair of socks or stockings that fit with sawdust and sew up the tops to keep the sawdust in. After taking off your shoes, and while they are still warm, stuff them with these curiously human forms. The shoes will keep their shape as the sawdust absorbs the moisture.

For small, delicate footwear wrap ribbon around whalebones or corset steels that are long enough to need bending to fit into the shoes.

Tips from the
OLD HOUSEWIVES

Fountain pens

Does anyone use a fountain pen these days? The way to clean one is to unscrew all the parts and soak them in vinegar for half an hour, then rinse them in warm water. They used to say that if you stuck pens into a potato when they were idle the nibs would not rust, but was this ever actually done?

The ubiquitous umbrella

Lost, stolen or strayed. This article has similarities with James James Morrison's mother in A. A. Milne's poem. The following is held to be a capital method of reviving a shabby silk umbrella. Put a tablespoonful of sugar into a basin and pour over it half a pint of boiling water. When the sugar has dissolved open the umbrella and with a sponge wash down the gores, starting at the ferrule.

If a black umbrella goes green take a sponge to it loaded with a cupful of cold strong tea to which about ten drops of ammonia have been added.

63

Cherish your aspidistra

When a new leaf appears, roll a piece of writing paper into a tube and place this over it. This will persuade the leaf to grow up quickly and straight as the light draws it up.

To make your plant look glistening with health, sponge the leaves – tops and undersides – with warm soapy water once a fortnight. If it looks sickly, try pushing a rusty nail into the soil and keep it well watered. The iron in the nail could help to feed the soil.

Almost everlasting flowers

Would you believe that cut flowers can be kept fresh a long time if their stems are put in a potato? Bore holes with a skewer and fix in the flowers. Stand the potato in a vase; no water is required. Another, more credible, method is to cut off a small piece of the stem every day and split the ends an inch or two if they are hard and woody. Add a little salt and soda to the water.

Fire-friendly economies

Save the cork from your bottles, or a cinder, soak it in a jar full of paraffin and use it to light or liven up a fire.

Recycle old paper (newspapers, comics, paper bags, etc.) to profit yourself rather than the council. Soak them in water in the kitchen sink or the bath until reduced to a pulp. Squeeze handfuls into balls and roll them in coal dust. They will burn beautifully.

Dry orange, lemon and grapefruit skins in the oven. They give out great heat as well as a delicious smell.

Candle odds and ends

A way of using up candle ends is to melt them in a saucer and draw some short lengths of string through the warm wax. When set you have some useful tapers for lighting the fire.

Wax that happens on clothes or upholstery is not as serious as it might at first seem. An old wrinkle was to put a little turpentine on the offending encrustation and let it soak in for half an hour. Then rub it and what remains will have turned into manageable dry "crumbs". Now we are more inclined to use newspaper or blotting paper and iron over it to soak up the wax. With velvet, hold the iron a little distance away so as not to flatten the pile.

A most excellent bed-warmer and other notions

Eat a bag of cherries and wash and dry the stones. Make a flannel bag. Heat the stones in a hot oven for a few minutes. Then put them in the bag and tie it up. It should stay hot all night.

Remember that a rubber hot-water bottle should never be put away flat so that the sides rest against each other as that increases the likelihood that the rubber will perish. Blow into the bottle and quickly screw up the stopper, leaving a little air inside.

And by the way, don't throw away an old hot-water bottle. Cut off the neck and thick rims, leaving two flat pieces of rubber. One piece will make two soles for wearing inside thin walking shoes; the other half (if covered with black sateen) will make a useful kneeling mat for searching the floor for pins and needles (or a contact lens).

Mistress of the wardrobe

Clothes, from toe to top hat

Yet another of the housewife's routine tasks would be to look after everyone's clothes. In this instance she would be doing the duties of a valet for a man and a lady's maid for herself. Nobody seems to have suggested what to do about teenage scruff. Perhaps it didn't exist in the old days.

Boots and shoes

To make boots waterproof (though they won't polish up very well afterwards) it was recommended that you treat the uppers to a coating made up of two parts beeswax to one part mutton fat, melted. Put this on in the evening and wipe the leather the next morning. (Mutton is now generally dressed up as lamb. Lamb fat would presumably do just as well.) Varnish the soles to keep out the damp. If shoes squeak, or creak, making clandestine activity impossible, soak them in salt and water and leave them overnight in linseed oil.

To dry boots, stuff them with oats or balls of newspaper and put them in a warm place for a day or two.

Boots and shoes that have not been worn for some time are apt to stiffen and lose their elasticity. To purge them of this bad habit, wash the leather with warm water and then dose it with castor oil.

To get rid of stains on brown boots – possibly black boots as well – a piece of lemon rubbed over them before they were polished was said to dispose of the problem. The inside of a banana skin used to be a favourite brown polish. Light-coloured shoes could do with rubbing over with a petrol and bran paste. Leave this to dry for ten minutes, then shake it off and dust with a clean damp cloth.

Clean suede shoes by rubbing them over with some sandpaper.

Never, never clean patent-leather shoes with ordinary shoe polish. Dip a rag in a little petrol, rub them well and polish with a soft rag. To look after patent leather give it a beauty treatment of sweet oil, and when things get really bad give them a surreptitious coat of black enamel paint

It is not generally known that bootlaces, if they are slightly (or lightly) waxed, do not easily come untied.

Gloves, to clean

There was a lot of fussing about gloves in the old days: when to wear them, when to take them off, what kind and what colour they should be. So, there were very precise instructions on how to treat them.

"How small these gloves make ones hand look!!"

 White kid gloves. If very slightly soiled rub with cream of tartar. Stronger stains may need to be treated with benzine and when dry rubbed with breadcrumbs.

 Suede gloves. Rub well with fuller's earth except in the case of white suede, when dry pipeclay should be used instead.

 Light kid gloves. Take a saucer of skimmed milk, some good hard soap and a piece of flannel, and spread the gloves on a clean towel, smoothing out the creases. Dip the flannel in the milk and rub a little soap on it, then rub the gloves, working downwards from the wrists. Rinse the flannel frequently but on no account rinse the gloves. Lay them out on a towel in the shape of a normal human being.

 Chamois leather gloves. Soak them for quarter of an hour in lukewarm soapy water to which a teaspoonful of ammonia has been added to each quart of water. Squeeze and squish them until all the dirt has been released into the water. Rinse and press them between the folds of a towel then dry them in the open air, giving them a rub every now and again to prevent *rigor mortis* setting in.

Astrakhan collars and cuffs

Now here's an ingenious idea for repairing one of your forbear's heavy overcoats with posh trimmings. Find an old hand-knitted sock or stocking of an appropriate colour and unravel the knitting. What you will find yourself with is a bundle of curly wool. With a large-eyed needle do a running stitch over the worn part, leaving loops after every stitch.

Folding, storing and packing

There is an approved way of treating every garment of male and female attire. The crumpled, hard-done-by look may be fashionable in some circles but it never used to be in our grandparents' and great-grandparents' day. You never saw a dress that had the appearance of seaweed or a bowler hat with a dent in it.

Make sure that anything with shoulders that spends its off-duty hours on a hanger has the centre of the neck or collar at the crook of the hanger otherwise the lopsidedness could become a permanent disability. Arms should fall to the front, as in life. Try not to leave tennis balls, etc., in pockets as their shape might be long-lasting.

Lay shirts and jerseys in a cupboard in terraces so that you can review them easily. Never yank one out from the bottom or middle but place the upper ones to one side. Fold shirts at the waist and ties at the neck.

Tissue paper is essential for proper, old-fashioned packing, in which shoes were never to be discovered on top of the suitcase. In fact, to be correct, they travelled in individual bags made of felt.

Material advice

- **Buckskin** Clean white buckskin with damp pipeclay. Shake it off once it has dried.

- **Chiffon** Wash chiffon in warm soap suds and rinse in water with a dash of ammonia. It will dry with wrinkles but don't be afraid. Iron over a cloth.

- **Satin** Remove water stains by rubbing gently with tissue paper in a circular motion.

- **Silk** Wash in a mixture of soft soap, honey and gin. Rinse in potato water to stiffen. Do not wring.

- **Suede** Renovate a suede bag with emery paper and brush very well with a soft brush.

- **Taffeta** Clean taffeta by soaking it in salt and water, then washing in soapy water. To stiffen add half a teaspoonful of borax to the rinsing water. Do not wring, and iron while damp.

- **Velvet** Clean with a solution made up of one part ammonia to eight parts water heated up. Dry by holding the article inside out in front of the fire. Fluff up the pile by holding the item inside out over boiling water or the steam from a kettle.

Nicotian notion

To get rid of the smell of tobacco on clothes it's quite a good idea to hang them up in the bathroom when you're having a bath and steam them. But let them dry properly before putting them away — or on.

The matter of hats

Wash a lady's straw hat with soap and water, rinse, air-dry and treat with white of egg beaten to a froth to stiffen it.

Clean a white felt hat with a paste of powdered calcined magnesia and water, or pipeclay.

When this has been on for a day or two brush it off. (Felt hats are easily marked by rainspots.)

Feathers can be washed in ordinary soapy water and shaken dry.

A gentleman's top hat also suffers in the rain, taking away its gloss and leaving it with spots. Wipe it dry as soon as possible and brush it with a soft camel-hair brush in the proper direction. (Don't ruffle it, in other words.) A gentle passing over with specially shaped flat irons – one for the side and one for the curl of the brim – should bring back its former splendour.

Black chip hats, which used to be very fashionable for men, need to be given a treatment of powdered sealing wax mixed with spirits of wine or turpentine so that they keep their stiffness and shine.

In sickness and for health

Remedies and wrinkles

Coughs and sneezes, and other diseases, required the attention of the housewife, either before or in the absence of supposedly superior counsel. She was relied upon to have a store of remedies, some of them inherited and some of them probably of her own invention.

Doses (or overdoses) of castor oil seem to have been administered not only for constipation – which was thought to be at the root of a great many ailments – but for a multitude of other problems, including a threatened cold. Cold baths and opium were also on the suggestions list.

Taking care of herself involved paying attention not only to her health but to her appearance. The housewife was supposed to magic away all the visible signs of her labours, emerging at the end of the day with perfectly white hands and a face without lines or wrinkles.

Don't bother the sick

- Don't contradict a sick person, interfere with anything he is doing or interrupt when he is speaking.

- Never lean against, sit upon or shake the bed upon which a sick person is lying.

- Never read to the sick except when they ask it; then read what they want, not what you think they ought to want, slowly and distinctly.

- Don't whisper or appear to be discussing the condition of a sick person just beyond the range of his hearing.

- Avoid wearing an expression of deep concern or one that intimates the proximity of death in the presence of a sick person.

- Give a little variety to the room by occasionally changing things. If flowers are liked, get them, but beware of the effect of very sweet perfumes.

- Never leave untasted food at the patient's bedside. The sight of that which is not craved is repellant.

- Remember that sick people are not necessarily mad.

Colds

Remedies for colds are almost as common as colds themselves. Most famous of them all is the mustard bath. Threatened colds and chills were supposed to depart immediately if the patient sat with his feet in a pail of hot water laced with mustard or immersed himself completely in a mustard bath.

A comforting gargle for a sore throat used to be concocted by adding a tablespoonful of chilli vinegar, six sage leaves and a dessertspoonful of honey to a small glass of port and simmering it for five minutes. A refreshing drink for someone with a sore throat was made with two ounces of barberries, and half an ounce of violets infused in a quart of boiling water for half an hour. This was sweetened with honey and decanted, and it was recommended that several glasses of it should be drunk during the day. Strawberries could be added when they were in season. Gargling with salt and water was considered efficacious.

To relieve irritation and congestion in the nose plug the nostrils with cotton wool recently dipped in glycerine.

Relief from hoarseness could, possibly, be obtained by dipping a flannel in hot water, sprinkling turpentine on it and laying it on the chest. For a cough, boil together half a cup of treacle and a piece of butter the size of a walnut and squeeze into this the juice of a lemon.

The grand-sounding Royal Posset for a cold, to be drunk hot just before going to bed, is made by mixing a tablespoonful of groats, or porridge oats, with a wineglass of cold water and pouring this into a pan containing nearly half a pint of white wine (ordinary French) sweetened with honey and flavoured with a few cloves. It needs to be stirred while it boils, for six minutes.

Half a pint of boiling milk poured on a heaped teaspoonful of ground cinnamon, sweetened to taste, makes a good palliative drink.

"The best Doctors in the World are Dr Diet, Dr Quiet and Dr Merryman."
Jonathan Swift (1667–1745)

An ache of the head

Some say that a handkerchief dipped in vinegar and placed on the forehead is the very thing for a bad headache; others put their trust in a freshly made cup of tea containing two cloves. Bathing the nape of the neck with near-boiling water is another suggestion; putting a pinch of salt on the tongue, followed ten minutes later by a drink of cold water, is one more.

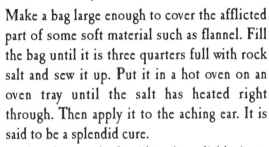

An ache of the ear

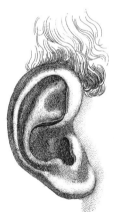

Make a bag large enough to cover the afflicted part of some soft material such as flannel. Fill the bag until it is three quarters full with rock salt and sew it up. Put it in a hot oven on an oven tray until the salt has heated right through. Then apply it to the aching ear. It is said to be a splendid cure.

Another method said to be reliable is to roast an onion, take out the centre and put the point of this into the ear for an hour or two.

An ache of the tooth

An old-fashioned remedy for this is made by breaking up four poppy-heads and pouring over them two pints of boiling water. Boil for ten minutes, then add two ounces of camomile flowers and boil for another five minutes. Strain off the liquid and bathe the face frequently or dip a flannel into it and apply it externally (and this is important) to the part affected.

Smoking a pipe of tobacco and caraway seeds was a more masculine way of quelling the pain.

Cures for the hiccups

Drink half a teaspoonful of vinegar and hold the hands above the head for a minute or two. Munch a lump of sugar soaked in vinegar. Or, close each ear with the first finger and recruit someone to hold a glass of liquid so a little may be drunk. Some say that drinking from a glass backwards effects a cure.

Hints on First Aid
(or perhaps what not to do)

"If poisoned, take of mustard, a tablespoon,
In a cup of warm water, and swallow right soon.
For burns try borax, and a wet bandage too;
If blistered, then oil and dry flannel will do.
For children's convulsions, warm baths are the rule
With castor-oil dose, but keep the head cool.
Give syrup of ipecac when croup is in store.
For fainting stretch patient right flat on the floor.
To soak in cold water is best for a sprain.
Remember these rules, and 'twill save you much pain."

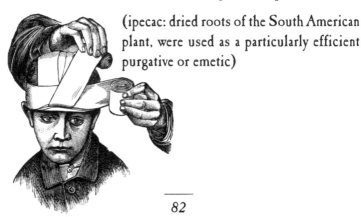

(ipecac: dried roots of the South American plant, were used as a particularly efficient purgative or emetic)

Hysterics

Young Victorian women of a nervous disposition, particularly unmarried women, were much prone to fits of hysteria. They happened much less often in married women, it was noticed, and rarely in men.

The symptoms were various. They included a pain as if a nail were being driven into the head, a pain on the left side that rose gradually until it reached the throat, then giving the patient the sensation of a pellet being held there and threatening to suffocate her, and episodes of crying, laughing or screaming, by which time she was generally insensible.

One of the most important details of the treatment was to loosen the patient's stays. As soon as she was able to swallow, twenty drops of sal volatile in a little water were to be administered. For someone with a strong constitution a plain diet was recommended, and occasional doses of castor oil; for those of a weaker, more delicate constitution, a nourishing diet, gentle exercise, cold baths, a dose of myrrh and aloes pills at night and compound iron pills twice a day. In every case, amusing the mind and avoiding all causes of over-excitement were believed to be of service in bringing about a permanent cure.

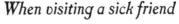

When visiting a sick friend

Never enter a sick room after a game of tennis or if you are in a perspiration, for the moment your body cools it is in a state likely to absorb the infection and give you the disease.

Never visit the sick room with an empty stomach as this also disposes the system more readily to receive the contagion.

In attending a sick person place yourself close to a door or window, breathing the air before it reaches the bed of the diseased person or the fireplace. The fire draws the infectious vapour in that direction and you would run much danger from breathing it.

Where the bee stings

The sting of a bee is acid and should be treated with washing soda or ammonia. The sting of a wasp is alkaline and should be treated with vinegar or with a blue bag. In both cases the bruised leaf of a poppy may give immediate relief, or damp tobacco applied to the sting.

Sting of the gnat, midge and mosquito

To prevent gnat and midge bites sprinkle your stockings with violet powder mixed with a small amount of white pepper. Dab mosquito bites with a solution of carbolic 1:20 to which a little eau de Cologne has been added. Four to five ounces will last the whole summer. (Never go to Africa or India without a bottle of this mixture.)

"Itch is more intolerable than smart"

Distinctions between apoplexy and drunkenness

Mrs Beeton's advice, word for word, was to take into account the following points when making a home diagnosis of these two conditions:

1. The known habits of the person.
2. The fact of a person who was perfectly sober and sensible a little time before, being found in a state of insensibility.
3. The absence, in apoplexy, of the smell of drink on applying the nose to the mouth.
4. A person in a fit of apoplexy cannot be roused at all; in drunkenness he mostly can, to a certain extent.

Hands and nails

These are extremities that suffer extremely from doing the cooking and housework. The advice used to be to take a wineglassful of eau de Cologne, half a cupful of lemon juice, scrape two cakes of white soap to a powder, mix well, mould and let it harden. Use this to give hands a once-desirable white complexion (before a sun tan became a fashion accessory) after a day's work. Or rub a ripe tomato over them two or three times a day and massage the juice into the skin. Some people used to keep a large jar of oatmeal beside the sink and washbasin. After drying their hands they would plunge them into the oatmeal and rub it into the skin.

Rubbing celery or a little mustard on the hands will take away the otherwise unmistakable smell of onions. And by the way, when peeling onions begin at the root end and peel upwards. This way the onion will be less likely to bring tears to your eyes.

Stained or discoloured fingernails should be soaked in a pint of warm water containing a dessertspoonful of lemon juice. Brittle nails can be treated by dipping them for a few minutes each day in lukewarm sweet oil.

To prevent lines forming on the face

This unattractive consequence of worrying over domestic matters must be avoided at all costs. After bathing with warm water and drying the face, rub it all over with the ball of the thumb to stimulate the circulation and strengthen the muscles. If there are deep lines running from the corners of the mouth to the corners of the nose, indicating an unacceptable degree of ageing, lay the thumb along them and then work from side to side.

Dandelion for the complexion

Eat the young leaves as a salad. Or bruise the dandelion root and squeeze out the juice, mix it in the proportion of two-thirds juice to one-third rectified spirits of wine and let it stand quite still for a week, then filter it through blotting-paper and a flannel bag. Take a teaspoonful of the potion two or three times a day. This was said to make it seem as though you led a healthy and well-ordered life.

Care of the hair

To prevent the hair from falling out, or to repair the damage caused by pulling the hair out in exasperation, wash the head every night using the following mixture: a teaspoonful of salt and a scruple (0.04 ounces) of quinine added to a pint of brandy, well shaken. Alternatively, put three onions without their skins into two pints of rum for twenty-four hours, take out the onions and rub the rum into the scalp every other day.

A cure for tired feet

This was a common complaint among housewives (and servants). An old remedy was to soak the feet in hot salt water for ten minutes and dry them thoroughly. Then, dust the feet and the inside of the stockings with boracic powder, one part, powdered starch, two parts, powdered French chalk, one part, to which is added a few drops of eucalyptus oil.

For a good night's sleep

Sleep is better than medicine, the saying goes; another is that one hour's sleep before midnight is worth three after, so don't stay up late.

The Victorians straightforwardly believed that the best preparation for sleep was an honest day's work, an abundance of exercise and fresh air, wholesome food and a clear conscience. They suggested having a cold bath before going to bed. This seems perverse advice and more likely to wake you up, though putting your feet alternately into hot and cold water improves the circulation, and going to bed with warm feet does make it easier to sleep. A draught of hot milk with a pinch of salt added at bedtime, or a teaspoonful of fresh lemon juice are other suggestions.

Counting sheep is an age-old remedy for insomnia. Is this because it is such a boring mental exercise that the brain would rather sign off for the night? You could try stuffing your pillow with hops.

On the hours of sleep:

"Nature requires five, custom gives seven, laziness takes nine, and wickedness eleven."

———

89

Domestic nuisances

What will rid me of these household pests?

Insects and other pestiferous creatures that invade the home are "the mere result of dirty, wasteful habits, and stupid neglect", admonished Mrs Haweis, who knew a thing or two about the art of housekeeping. Leave no crumbs, dregs, half-scoured bones or other scraps to entice them in, and apply to surfaces plentiful doses of carbolic. Mice and moth don't care for the smell of camphor and all insects, including earwigs, we are assured, dislike the smell of pennyroyal.

Ant counter-attack

A little green sage placed in ants' haunts sends them running, or leave a plate smeared with lard overnight and in the morning immerse the plate, which you will find covered with ants, in boiling water. Observe their walks, which are monotonously regular, and pepper them till they get tired of making new ones. Out of doors, quicklime scattered over their hills and watered will destroy them.

Tips from the
OLD HOUSEWIVES

Cockroaches and black beetles

Parings of cucumber positioned near their holes, or strong snuff (obtainable from all good tobacconists), will prevent their approach. The smell of burning potato peelings is said also to be very obnoxious to them, though you really need an open fire to carry out the procedure properly.

Cockroaches, will devour ground rice as though they had scrounged nothing for weeks. It swells up inside them and they die. So, if you don't think this is too cruel a plan, sprinkle some around. Another, supposedly infallible, method is to strew the roots of black hellebore at night in the places infested by these pests.

An impressively strategic way of exterminating beetles is to build staircases from strips of cardboard on which a raw onion has been rubbed and prop them against a jar, making sure that the tops are bent over the mouth. The jar is to be part-filled with black treacle (not golden syrup) and water. Beetles find this delicacy completely irresistible and, having climbed up a staircase, topple into the jar and are trapped.

House flies

These uninvited visitors torment with their persistent whirr and unforced landings, and they leave spots on furniture and lampshades. Some flies actually convince themselves that they are welcome and seem to be trying to make friends, repeatedly getting close and staring at you.

Combine half a spoonful of ground black pepper with a teaspoonful of brown sugar and a teaspoonful of cream. Leave the mixture in a room where flies are troublesome. Alternatively, put sweetened green tea in saucers about the place, a concoction that is poison to them. If you feel like making little bags of muslin, these, filled with cloves, are good for keeping them away.

An ingenious suggestion for achieving a fly-free zone involved tying a wineglass, broken at the base of the stem, to a pole long enough to reach the ceiling. After sunset or in the early morning, when flies are asleep, the trick was to hold the glass, half full of methylated spirits, under the flies. They would be poisoned by the fumes and drop into the glass. *Not* a time- or labour-saving method.

Soak a large bundle of leeks for five or six days in a bucket of water and wash picture and mirror frames with the liquid to deter flies from settling on them.

It is said with authority that flies particularly dislike elder leaves, walnut leaves and the smell of lavender, and that hanging up a fresh bunch of nettles in a window stops flies coming into the house from outdoors.

Bugs in your bed

These are *really* unwelcome creatures and difficult to trap. Bedrooms were often painted green or had green in the wallpaper because the colour contained arsenic as the pigment and bugs knew to avoid it. Treating the mattress with paraffin and boiling water was recommended by some people.

The moth

To take out winter woollies on the first cold day and find them full of holes is more than a minor disappointment. In the warm weather the creatures have been silently about their destructive business, attending especially to places where there are remnants of spilt food. This is normally on the front of the garment, just where a hole is most conspicuous. Camphor moth balls are the best-known preventative. Cedar shavings (used to wrap cigars), cloves and tobacco could be used, or Epsom salts tied up in little muslin bags. The printing ink on newspapers also acts as a deterrent, so it is a good idea to wrap woollens in newspaper when they are put away during the summer.

Should moths have the audacity to get into a piano, make up a mixture of turpentine, benzoline and lavender oil and squirt this inside the instrument: seven parts benzoline to one of turpentine, adding just a few drops of the lavender oil. If they make their way into the carpet put a damp cloth over the part they have been guzzling and go over it with a very hot iron. This should do for the eggs and grubs. To prevent them getting there in the first place sprinkle salt on the carpet before sweeping it.

Mice aren't all that nice

The sight of the tail of a mouse disappearing into the larder can bring on a fit of hysterics in some people – even women of the post-Victorian era (see *hysterics*). These creatures are the terrorists of the home.

Stop up mouse holes with soap and pepper or else corks dipped in turpentine or in water and cayenne pepper. Sprinkling the larder with the cayenne sometimes helps, and they have a strong aversion to peppermint, so try sprinkling oil or essence of peppermint about their holes. If you resort to a mousetrap remember that mice are partial to chocolate as well as cheese, so it depends which you would rather give away. A cat has always been the best answer to mice, especially a hungry one. If there is no resident Jerry to see off Tom, borrow a neighbour's.

"But mice and rats and such small deer
Have been Tom's food for seven long year."

Shakespeare

Rats

Seriously, to get rid of rats, "Place a large stone at the bottom of a barrel, add sufficient water to allow stone to show above enough for the rat to stand on. Cover the head of the barrel with stiff brown paper, sprinkled with cheese for the first night. The following night cut paper in the form of a cross, and add more cheese. The first rat falling in will get on the stone. His cries will soon attract the others, who will follow, and quickly drown."

How to discover a dead rat

I sincerely hope that you won't need to know the answer to this, but, if you do, try following these instructions. Capture half a dozen bluebottles (no clues as to how) and put them in a jar. Let the flies out in the room where you suspect the rat has met its death and sit down while they fly around (important). Within an hour they will have scented the suspect and will be buzzing round the spot. That is where your rat is. You can then take up the floorboard and put it to rest somewhere else.